Desert Scientists

By Patrick and Janet Lalley

A Harcourt Company

www.steck-vaughn.com

Copyright © 2002, Steck-Vaughn Company

ISBN 0-7398-4935-2

All rights reserved. No part of this book may be reproduced or utilized in any form or by any means, electronic or mechanical, including photocopying, recording, or by any information storage and retrieval system, without permission in writing from the publisher. Inquiries should be addressed to Copyright Permissions, Steck-Vaughn Company, P.O. Box 26015, Austin, TX 78755.

Printed and bound in the United States of America
1 2 3 4 5 6 7 8 9 10 WZ 05 04 03 02 01

Photo Acknowledgments
Corbis, cover
Digital Stock, 16, 31, 32, 41 (top)
Photo Network, 15; David N. Davis, title page; Henryk T. Kaiser, 6, 40 (top); Jim Schwabel, 22; Nancy Hoyt Belcher, 25; Hal Beral, 29; Esbin Anderson, 36; F. Armstrong, 39, 40 (bottom); Jeff Greenberg, 44
Visuals Unlimited/John Gerlach, 9, 41 (bottom); Jon Turk, 10; Charles McRae, 21, 26; Janine Pestel, 34

Content Consultants
Maria Kent Rowell
Science Consultant
Sebastopol, California

David Larwa
National Science Education Consultant
Educational Training Services
Brighton, Michigan

This book supports the National Science Standards.

Contents

What Is a Desert Biome? 5

A Scientist in the Chihuahuan Desert 13

Scientists in the Deserts of the United States . 19

What Does the Future Hold for Deserts? 35

Quick Facts 40

Glossary 43

Internet Sites 45

Useful Addresses 46

Books to Read 47

Index 48

This map shows where the major deserts in the world are.

What Is a Desert Biome?

The desert is a **biome**. A biome is a large region, or area, made of **communities**. A community is a group of certain plants and animals that live in the same place.

Communities in the same biome are alike in some ways. In the desert biome, for example, all plants and animals live with extremes. The desert is dry. It receives less than 10 inches (25 cm) of rain or snow each year. The desert also has extreme temperatures. It can be very hot or very cold.

There are more than 14 large desert areas in the world. Deserts cover 1/7 of Earth's surface. Most deserts are found north or south of the **equator**. The equator is an imaginary line that wraps around the middle of Earth.

 Wind sometimes blows sand into large dunes like these.

Kinds of Deserts

There are two kinds of deserts in the world. There are hot deserts and cold deserts. Cold deserts have long cold seasons and short warm seasons. Most deserts are hot deserts. Hot deserts are warm throughout most of the year.

What Are Deserts?

Deserts have very little water and extreme temperature changes. In some deserts, the temperature can change by 36° F (2° C) each day.

When many people think about deserts, they think of sand. Some deserts, however, have more than sand. Cold deserts can be covered by sand, gravel, fine clay, or rocky soil. They are deserts because they receive very little rain or snow. The average winter temperature in a cold desert is below 32° F (0° C). The summer temperature averages between 69° and 79° F (21° and 26° C).

Hot deserts have sand and rock formations. They can be covered by sand **dunes**. Sand dunes are mounds of sand made by blowing wind. Hot deserts are very warm all year round. In the summer, temperatures can reach 131° F (55° C) during the day. The nighttime temperature during the cold seasons can drop to 32° F (0° C).

Some of the most famous deserts have huge sand dunes. The wind moves the sand into many shapes and sizes. In the Sahara in north Africa, sand dunes sometimes move 60 feet (18 m) a year.

What Lives in Deserts?

Desert plants and animals adapted in order to live in the harsh **climate**. To be adapted means that something is a good fit for where it lives. Many plants and animals that live in deserts could not live in other biomes.

The hot desert is home to many plants. The most common plants in hot deserts are small shrubs and **cacti**. These plants can live in hot temperatures and with very little water.

Grasses and sagebrush are the most common plants in the cold desert. Cold desert plants can survive very cold temperatures. They can also live with little water.

Kangaroo rats, jackrabbits, snakes, and tortoises are found in hot deserts. These animals have ways to stay cool during the day. They also know how to find water to drink.

Animals in cold deserts have ways to stay warm. They also have ways to **conserve** water. To conserve means to save. Animals in cold deserts include bighorn sheep, lizards, and gerbils.

People also live in hot and cold deserts. In the United States, the cities of Las Vegas and

▲ **Kangaroo rats keep cool in deserts by hiding in holes in the ground during the day.**

Phoenix are located in hot deserts. Cities in cold deserts include Reno and Salt Lake City.

People called nomads also live in hot and cold deserts. Nomads have no permanent homes. Because nomads move around to find food and water for their herds, they often live in tents.

▲ People need to be careful not to damage deserts when traveling through them.

Why Are Deserts in Danger?

Deserts are special places. This might be hard to believe because deserts sometimes seem lifeless. But deserts are filled with plants and animals. People, however, are hurting desert habitats. A habitat is a place where an animal or plant usually lives. More people are moving to the desert. That means there is less room for the plants and animals that already live there. Many of the desert plants and animals are losing their homes.

People also harm the desert by using too much water. Sometimes the water cannot be replaced as fast as people use it. This leaves too little water for the plants and animals that live in the desert. People can also destroy desert habitats by driving bikes, cars, and trucks through them.

Global warming can also affect deserts. Global warming is a slow but measurable rise in temperatures across all of Earth. Changes in temperatures, even by a few degrees, can cause changes in weather patterns. These changes mean some deserts might receive more or less rain than they used to. Some might have higher or lower temperatures than usual. New weather patterns may affect or hurt some desert plants and animals.

This map shows the location of the Chihuahuan Desert where Michael Powell works.

United States

Mexico

Water
Chihuahuan Desert
Surrounding Land

A Scientist in the Chihuahuan Desert

Michael Powell is a scientist who works in the Chihuahuan Desert in the southwest United States and northern Mexico. Powell is a **biology professor** at Sul Ross University in Alpine, Texas. He has been studying the desert for almost 40 years.

The Chihuahuan Desert is 1,200 miles (1,931 km) long and 800 miles (1,287 km) wide. It stretches from southern New Mexico and Arizona to Mexico City, Mexico.

Powell believes that each desert is a beautiful place filled with plants and animals not found anywhere else. Powell became a scientist because he wanted to study all the different kinds of things that live in the desert.

Rain-Shadow Effect

The Chihuahuan Desert is dry because it is bordered by two mountain ranges. The rain-shadow effect keeps the area between the mountains dry. The rain-shadow effect happens when mountains block moving clouds. The clouds cool as they move upward. Cooler temperatures mean the clouds cannot hold as much water. Rain or other kinds of moisture fall on the windward side of the mountains. That means less moisture falls on the dry land on the other side of the mountains. In this case, the dry land is called the Chihuahuan Desert.

The Chihuahuan Desert has different elevations. Elevation is the distance between sea level and the highest point on land. Different elevations have different weather. Higher elevations are cooler and wetter than lower elevations. This means that many different kinds of plants live there.

Plants

Different plants grow in different elevations. Desert scrub grows in the lower areas. Desert scrub is the name for several kinds of small

▲ These are some of the many kinds of cacti that grow in the Chihuahuan Desert.

bushes, plants, and shrubs. Many different kinds of trees grow in the mountain areas.

There are more kinds of cacti in the Chihuahuan Desert than in any other desert. Many scientists believe that cacti first developed in the Chihuahuan Desert and then spread to other areas.

 Many colorful lizards live in the Chihuahuan Desert.

Animals

There are many animals in the Chihuahuan Desert. Tarantulas, scorpions, lizards, and snakes are common. The larger animals are usually nocturnal. That means they are active at night and sleep during the day. There are many coyotes, jackrabbits, and mice. Mountain lions also live in the desert. In northern Mexico, there are some wolves and bears as well.

Natural History

In 1964, Powell started planning the Chihuahuan Desert Research Institute. Today, people at the Institute research, or study the desert's natural history. Natural history is the study of science in an area. It includes the study of animals, plants, rocks, and minerals.

Powell spends a lot of time studying plants. He studies how plants affect each other. He also tries to find new kinds of plants. He teaches students and writes science articles to share what he learns with others. Powell thinks that his research helps other people understand the desert better. Better understanding can lead to conservation.

Powell believes that each desert is a beautiful place filled with plants and animals not found anywhere else. He started the Chihuahuan Desert Research Institute because he wanted to study all the different kinds of things that live there.

Scientists in the Deserts of the United States

Nancy Huntly works in the cold desert of the Great Basin. The Great Basin is an area of land that covers a huge part of the western United States.

Huntly is a professor of **ecology** at Idaho State University. Ecology is the study of how plants and animals in a community interact. She studies the ecology of parts of the cold desert in southeastern Idaho.

Huntly is a population biologist. She counts plants and animals and measures their birth and death rates. This information tells scientists whether the animals and plants are healthy or not. If the population becomes too low, the plants and animals are listed as endangered.

Studying Plants and Animals

While Huntly was in college, she helped discover something very interesting about black-tailed jackrabbits. She learned that the number of these rabbits increases about every 10 years.

She also learned that when it snows, these rabbits group together near sagebrush. Waste from the rabbits helps the sagebrush to grow. Waste is undigested food that leaves an animal's body in droppings. When they die, the rabbits keep helping the sagebrush to grow. Their bodies decompose, or break down, into nutrients. Nutrients are materials that living things need to stay healthy and to grow. This means the rabbits help keep sagebrush alive. Huntly says that this discovery surprised many scientists.

Huntly also studies how soil and weather affect plants and animals in the desert. She does experiments to try to figure out how water, soil, and plants affect each other. To do this, she uses special machines that measure nutrients in soil.

Huntly also raises plants in special buildings to study how they grow. To study plants

▲ Huntly learned that the black-tailed jackrabbit population increases every 10 years.

outside, she sometimes builds fences to protect plants from animals. This helps her figure out how animals affect the plants. Then, Huntly puts the information she collects into computers. Finally, she uses the computers to study the information.

One way people can keep deserts healthy is by walking on paths so plants are not harmed.

How Do People Affect Cold Deserts?

Huntly says that cold deserts are important to the culture of the western United States. Culture is a group's way of life, ideas, customs, and traditions. The Great Basin area has given ideas to many writers and artists, for example.

The Great Basin is a large area, but it is threatened by humans. Desert plants and animals are dying out for several reasons. Huntly says that cold deserts in the United States have become smaller because people have moved into them. People use the land to build homes, roads, and stores. Some farmers let their cows and sheep eat the desert plants. People also introduce new plants to the area that are not desert plants. All these things change and threaten the cold desert.

Huntly hopes that her research will help people understand cold deserts better. Knowing more about desert ecology will help people live as a part of it. Huntly believes that people can learn how to live in the cold desert without damaging it.

 Did you know the driest place on Earth is the Atacama Desert? This desert is located in the country of Chile in South America. It is believed to have received no more than about 0.05 inches (1 mm) of rain per year for 400 years.

Engineering in the Desert

Huntly and the scientists she works with hope their work will help conserve the cold deserts. They believe that learning how humans affect nature will help people live on the land without destroying it. The scientists call their work "ecological engineering." Engineering means to use a plan to make something happen.

As ecological engineers, the scientists do several things. For example, they look for ways cows and sheep can graze in the cold desert without hurting the plants. They also look for ways to use native plants to slow down soil **erosion**. Erosion happens when water, wind, or ice carry soil away. Finding ways for people to build roads and homes without hurting the desert is also important to Huntly and the other desert scientists.

Ecological engineers help plan the best ways to build roads through deserts.

Muth walks in the desert to find lizards like this one to study.

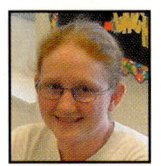

What Are Other Kids Saying?
Janine Phelps is a sixth grade student. She believes that science "opens a window to the world." She says that it does not matter where you live because you can help save deserts as long as you have a passion for what you are trying to protect. She especially wants to save the animals that live in the dry deserts.

The Lizard Scientist

Allan Muth did not know what he wanted to do when he grew up. He got out of high school and went to a community college. There, he took a class in biology that changed his life. Muth decided that he wanted to be a biologist. A biologist is a scientist who studies living things. Muth went to school for several more years. He now has a doctorate, which is the highest degree a person can earn.

Today, Muth is the director of a desert research center at a university. Muth works in the Coachella Valley, near Palm Desert, California. He is really interested in lizards. He spends a lot of time walking in the desert looking for them.

Studying Lizards

Muth and other scientists catch lizards and mark them. They also find lizards that have already been caught and released. They learn a lot by measuring how much these lizards have grown and how far they have traveled since they were caught last.

Muth says that sometimes he feels like a kid sent to find new things in the desert. Even with all of his training, there are days, Muth says, when he feels like he knows almost nothing. "That is because there is so much to learn in the desert," he says.

"The desert is a very hard place to live in. Learning about the plants and animals there teaches us what it is like to live in extreme conditions," says Muth. "That is why it is so important to study them."

Information scientists gather about animal and plant adaptation might help them figure out better ways for people to live in extreme conditions. Then, people might learn how to live in deserts without harming the **environment**.

Muth studies how much lizards grow and where they travel.

The Bat Scientist

Like the other scientists you have read about, Doug Allen really likes what he does. He is a wildlife biologist. He works in the deserts of southern California and southwestern Arizona where he gets to be outside and to work with animals. The desert has many animals that are not found anywhere else. Allen keeps track of birds, butterflies, and toads. He especially likes to study bats. "One scientist can spend his or her whole life trying to answer one question," Allen says. "That is because one question almost always leads to another." Allen says that is what science is all about.

The deserts of the southwest United States are very hot during the day. The temperature often rises above 100° F (37.8° C). At night, it can get very cold. Allen spends many nights camping in the desert, looking for animals. He says he has to be ready for just about anything.

Allen camps in the desert at night to look for bats. He goes into mines and tunnels. He carries mountain climbing gear and special tools that let him see when it is dark out. He also carries other special tools that help him find bats.

Doug Allen especially likes to study bats like this one.

Doug Allen keeps track of birds that live in the desert, such as this vulture.

Work in the Desert

Allen has many interesting stories about working in the desert. One time, he was exploring an old mine shaft. He was 600 feet (183 m) below the ground. There, he found a bat that another scientist had tagged in the 1960s. The bat was very old. Allen was very happy to find a bat that had lived so long.

Allen studies how bats live in the desert. He wants to know what they eat, when they eat, and where they live. He also wants to know if desert bats sleep through the cold season. Sleeping deeply through the cold season is called hibernating.

Like Huntly, Allen thinks that people are the biggest danger to the desert. More and more people are moving to the deserts in California. "That means the animals and plants that already live there are in trouble," says Allen. "If something is not done to control people, some of the desert plants and animals might be lost forever," he says. Allen hopes that the more scientists know, the more they can help people protect delicate biomes like the deserts.

Today people are harming deserts by building large cities in desert areas.

What Does the Future Hold for Deserts?

The future of deserts depends on people. People who live in deserts can help save them in different ways. Planting desert grasses is one way to help. The grasses help stop wind erosion. The plants' roots hold the desert sand together and stop the wind from blowing it away.

People can also take care of desert plants by driving only on paved roads. People who leave paved roads often run over and kill desert plants.

Farmers and ranchers can also help save the desert. They can keep their animals from eating the plants other animals use for food.

These desert rock formations are protected because they are part of Death Valley National Park.

FUN FACT Did you know there are different kinds of sand dunes? Long ridges of sand called seif dunes form in the direction of the prevailing wind. Prevailing means the way something happens most of the time. A prevailing wind is wind that blows in one direction most of the time. What happens when the wind blows from all directions? Then, the sand dunes do not have a regular shape.

Where Are Deserts Protected the Best?

Deserts are protected best in national parks. A national park is a park that is owned and protected by the government. In a desert national park, desert animals and plants are protected from harm by people, livestock, cars, and trucks.

In the United States, there are many desert national parks where people can visit, including the Death Valley National Park and the Grand Canyon National Park. The Great Basin National Park includes a cold desert. It was made into a national park in 1986. It covers about 77,109 acres (31,205 ha) of the western United States.

The Endangered Desert Tortoise

One of the **endangered** desert animals is the desert tortoise. Endangered means the animal is in danger of becoming extinct. The number of tortoises is dropping fast. In some places, desert tortoises have disappeared completely.

There are several reasons desert tortoises are endangered. Much of the tortoises' habitat has been lost. People have built highways, houses, and farms where tortoises used to live. People have also captured desert tortoises as pets. This is now against the law.

Desert tortoises need people's help to survive. You can help by contacting the Desert Tortoise Preserve Committee. This group's address and website are listed in the back of this book. This group helps teach people about saving the tortoise and about creating preserves where they will be safe.

Cars put desert tortoises in danger. Drivers sometimes run over the tortoises by accident.

Quick Facts

The largest desert in the world is the Sahara Desert in northern Africa. It covers an area of about 3.5 million square miles (9 million sq. km). Sand dunes cover large parts of the Sahara.

The Great Basin Desert is the only cold desert in the United States.

The largest desert tortoise is about 15 inches (38.1 cm) in length.

Desert animals rarely drink water. They get their water from the food they eat.

Lizards and snakes get their water from the insects and animals they eat.

Camels have long eyelashes to keep desert sand out of their eyes. They can also close their nostrils so sand does not get in their noses.

Desert rats and mice get all of the water they need from the seeds and plants they eat.

The damage that an off-road vehicle causes in the desert will last longer than the driver's lifetime.

On the following pages, you can find sources of information that tell how to help save deserts.

Glossary

biology (bye-OL-uh-jee)—the scientific study of living things

biome (BYE-ohm)—large regions, or areas, in the world that have similar climates, soil, plants, and animals

cacti (KAK-tye)—the word for more than one cactus. Cacti are desert plants adapted to living in dry climates. Some cacti have thick trunks and sharp thorns, which are modified leaves.

climate (KLYE-mit)—the usual weather patterns in a place

community (kuhm-YOO-nih-tee)—different species of plants and animals living together in a habitat

conserve (kuhn-SURV)—to save or protect something

dune (DOON)—a sand hill made by the wind

ecology (ee-KOL-uh-jee)—the study of how living things interact with each other and their environment

endangered (en-DAYN-jurd)—an animal or plant that is danger of dying out

environment (en-VYE-ruhn-muhnt)—all the living and nonliving things that affect life on Earth

equator (i-KWAY-tur)—an imaginary line around the middle of Earth, halfway between the North and South Poles

erosion (i-ROH-zhuhn)—when water, wind, or ice pick up and carry away Earth materials

professor (pruh-FESS-ur)—a teacher of the highest rank at a college or university

Internet Sites

Chihuahuan Desert
http://www.nasa.utep.edu/chih/chihdes.htm
Find information about the special plants and animals that live in the Chihuahuan Desert.

Desert Tortoise Preserve Committee
http://www.tortoise-tracks.org
You can learn more about desert tortoises and how to save them at this site.

DesertUSA
http://www.desertusa.com/index.html
This site describes different deserts in the United States.

The Great Basin National Park
http://www.great.basin.national-park.com
Learn about the land, wildlife, and features of the Great Basin at this site.

Useful Addresses

Death Valley National Park
P.O. Box 579
Death Valley, CA 92328

Desert Tortoise Preserve Committee
4067 Mission Inn Avenue
Riverside, CA 92502

Great Basin National Park
Baker, NV 89311-9702

Mojave Desert State Parks
43779 15th Street West
Lancaster, CA 93534

Books to Read

Barrett, Norman S. *Deserts.* New York: Franklin Watts, 1989.
Learn all about the special features of deserts.

Bramwell, Martyn. *Deserts.* London: Franklin Watts, 1987.
Explore the climate, wildlife, and geography of deserts in this book.

Morris, Neil. *Deserts.* New York: Crabtree, 1996.
Discover information about deserts and some of the different deserts of the world.

Steele, Christy. *Deserts.* New York: Raintree Steck-Vaughn, 2000.
This book describes the geography, animals, and plants of deserts as well as people's affect on the biome.

Index

Allen, Doug, 30, 33

bats, 30, 33
biome, 5, 8, 33

cacti, 8, 15
Chihuahuan Desert, 13, 14, 15, 16
cold desert, 6, 7, 8, 19, 23, 24, 37
community, 5

dunes, 7, 37

ecological engineering, 24
equator, 5
erosion, 24, 35

Great Basin, 19, 23, 37

hot desert, 6, 7, 8
Huntly, Nancy, 19–21, 23–24, 33

lizards, 8, 16, 27, 28

Muth, Allan, 27–28

national park, 37
nocturnal, 16
nomads, 9
nutrient, 20

Powell, Michael, 13, 17

tortoises, 8, 38